Common Law

By Lord Loveday Ememe and available from Lulu and Amazon

The constitution and policing

Heresy

Starfleet

The Supernatural

Creation

Deterrence

Stalking

The Media

Adam

Criminal Responsibility

The Wicked

www.lulu.com

Copyright ©Lord Loveday Ememe 2015

The author asserts the moral right to be recognized as the author of this work.
ISBN: 978-1-326-24450-7

Table of Contents

1 Tradition

2 Witchcraft or Wizardry

3 A legal person protected by law

4 Torture

5 Author's notes

6 Author's biography

7 Bibliography

1. Tradition

The tradition of the United Kingdom is based on the relationship between the nobles and the working class and it is based on this relationship that a real civilized society is created.

The history or tradition of the United Kingdom refers to the nobility as the ruling class. A real noble person is of a civil constitution without supernatural powers and senses.

The working class are responsible for making sure that all the domestic and financial needs of the nobles are fulfilled and the nobles are responsible for governing or ruling the country. The noble person is pivotal to the creation of a civilized society. To meet the special needs of a noble person is the sacred formula for the creation of paradise which is another word for civilization or heaven. The word civilization is derived from the sacred constitution of the noble civil person. The noble civil person is a living human being without supernatural powers and senses.

Tradition in the United Kingdom and in most cultures around the world requires the working class to bow or prostrate to a noble person. This requirement contrary to the political propaganda of the working class is not oppressive or domineering but is for the security, physical and mental wellbeing of the noble person. The working class are supernatural beings and the nobles are civil beings without supernatural powers and senses. There are very serious security and health concerns for nobles as a consequence of supernatural beings establishing informal relationships with nobles or familiarity. Informality or familiarity will inevitably lead to the god complex or superiority complex disease or trait associated with the supernatural constitution; this will lead to the constant unlawful supernatural interference with nobles supernaturally for one stupid reason after another which will cumulate to make the lives of the nobles hell unlawfully.

The traditional requirements to bow or to prostrate serve as medication and meditation that help supernatural beings exercise self-control. While in the process of bowing or prostrating the supernatural being only speaks when spoken to directly by the noble person. Tradition confirms that contrary to the current unlawful abominable practices it is the supernatural uncivilized constitution that needs to be regulated and not the already civilized noble constitution of real nobles. The civil noble constitution has been created or constituted already sacredly regulated for a sacred regulatory purpose so no further regulation of this noble constitution is required or permitted. The regulatory functions of the noble constitution have direct and indirect applications. This is further emphasized by the noble constitution being constituted to have allergic reactions to supernaturalism. Supernaturalism is lawlessness. When supernatural beings the working class defy this sacred determination and attempt to regulate the noble constitution it is for unlawful political purposes to hide, misrepresent their unlawful abominable practices that are in violation of some or all the indirect regulatory orders of the noble constitution. In some cases these abominations by supernatural beings are attempts to cover up not meeting or fulfilling their obligations to the state, the noble constitution. Examples of the failures of supernatural beings to satisfy their obligations to the state are the use of electricity and gas for cooking and heating during winter and the use of nuclear power stations for electricity, they are extremely dangerous and put lives and the security of this planet in danger.

The indirect regulatory functions of the civil noble constitution start from birth or in Lord Adam's case from when he was created. The educational requirements including the method of education of the civil noble constitution is dependent on holy or righteous surroundings in order not to corrupt or compromise the development of the noble person.

Traditionally nobles are educated separately from the working class supernatural beings and healthcare provided separately, this will suggest that it is wrong to link the fate of nobles with supernatural beings because of their hostile self-destructive traits.

The trap set for supernatural beings as a type of security sifting process for the protection of real nobles which has the effect of establishing and maintaining peace and security on this planet and beyond is the active indirect regulatory duties of a real noble person from birth. This confirms why traditionally the working class approach nobles with extreme caution even in their capacities as healthcare providers, tutors etcetera. There are traditionally no excuses accepted for the mental or physical abuse of a noble person by a working class person. Traditionally the working class are responsible for manual labour while the nobles are responsible for administration or governing. Traditionally no working class person gets involved in administrative work, they are permitted only as assistants to a noble person or noble persons. In these roles as assistants to nobles in administrative work they definitely do not get anywhere close to the huge sums of money nobles get. This simply means that because of the huge differences between the civil and supernatural constitutions the huge sums of money nobles get compensates for the differences. Traditionally it is accepted that nobles give more to the peace and security of a country and should be rewarded accordingly, this is true and not obvious to conventional observation when applied to real noble persons and the real working class.

The bible identifies companionship as only meant for the civil noble constitution. The bible implies that companionship is the only type of recreational activity meant for the civil noble constitution. The tradition and history of England identified the problem Lord Adam had with the creation of Eve as his companion, females originally uncivilized from birth or creation can be trained to be suitable companions for a real noble person, Ladies in waiting.

Given that companionship is meant for the civil noble constitution and remains a constant civil right, the indirect regulatory functions of the civil noble constitution that operate as a gauge will make the determination that if there are no suitable supernatural female companions for the noble Lord it implies that the world is in a state of anarchy because of the lawless practices of supernatural beings. The Vulcans a fictional alien species in the star trek television series and movies by Gene Roddenberry are supernatural humanoids that try to live by reason and logic to avoid the crisis of their past when they tried to destroy each other because of their uncivilized constitutions similar to the situation in present day earth. This is something developed in these series and movies by supernatural beings that are aware of the out of control practices of their peers. I believe that common law developed through tradition and history in the United Kingdom if applied correctly to the differences between the civil and supernatural constitutions provides the opportunity for supernatural beings to live by reason and logic. Civil beings, nobles, represent reason and logic. Most of the Vulcans are science officers in the television series and movies; it is through science like the Garden of Eden that an advanced civilization can be created and not supernaturalism. The bible instructs that a distinction must be made between the civil and supernatural constitutions from birth or creation, even when the civil and supernatural constitutions are born from the same womb and the civil noble constitution must be identified as king with the rights and privileges. The correct identification and distinction must be made in order to prevent the world from descending into total anarchy as is the state of the world today.

The bible, international and domestic legislations bar supernatural beings from direct or indirect contact or communication with civil beings. Common law has provided guidelines or protocols for limited situations when contact or communication might be necessary to prevent the unlawful horrific situation that occurred in the Garden of Eden that led to the unlawful undermining of the sacred authority of Lord Adam by out of control power tripping supernatural beings.

The indirect regulatory functions or authority of the noble constitution protect the noble constitution from supernatural political manipulations, direct or indirect force or threat, any type of bullying by out of control power tripping supernatural beings.

Common law confirms that political supernatural reassurances do not protect the civil noble constitution from the hostile uncivilized nature of the supernatural constitution; goodwill is a contradiction when applied to the supernatural constitution. As a consequence common law has provided guidelines for supernatural beings when trying to initiate contact with nobles. Bowing and prostrating are protocols developed by common law for the security of the noble person; they ensure that supernatural beings are always reminded to know their place when in direct or indirect contact with real nobles or confronted with the affairs of real noble persons.

Common law protocols required of the supernatural working class when they have contact with real nobles serve as a reminder that nobles do not have political emotions associated with criminal responsibility because real nobles are not criminally responsible. Common law protocols are linked to the duty of care owed to real nobles by supernatural beings which must be delivered in a civilized legal manner that comply with the indirect regulatory instructions of real nobles that establish and maintain universal peace and security. The method of delivery is very important which must comply with the real health and safety standards, it must be quick. The challenge for supernatural beings is how to scientifically satisfy the needs of real nobles without the use of supernatural powers and senses to comply with the indirect regulatory order of a real noble.

This will suggest that money is meant for real nobles as a regulatory tool as an orderly method of accessing goods and services and as a punishment tool through the taxation of supernatural beings until they have fulfilled their obligations to the state the real nobles through scientific or technological advancements. This will also suggest that supernatural beings are not allowed to have more money than real nobles in order not to defeat its regulatory purpose.

Tradition or common law confirms that the nobility or the ruling class are born or created to rule, this is not vulnerable to supernatural political manipulations aimed at avoiding their actions being regulated. This distinction has been reinforced by international and domestic legislations that identify only the civil noble constitution as a legal person or legal persons with legal rights including the legal right to rule. The legal definition of a person does not include the supernatural constitution even if the supernatural being is pretending to be a real noble person. Common law identifies this practice of the working class pretending to be a noble person or persons as a serious crime against the state.

Common law has provided through the sacred protocols, rights and privileges for the noble constitution the necessary checks and balances for the security of the noble lord given the massive differences between the real nobles and supernatural beings. Supernatural beings have no margin for error, any deviation from these protocols, rights and privileges of the noble lord will constitute making the lives of nobles hell unlawfully which will automatically trigger the noble lord's sacred legal right of vengeance the condemnation to hell of the wicked as described in the bible. This has been reemphasized through common law's description of the protocols, rights and privileges at each stage of a country's development.

The bible confirms that a distinction must be made between the civil and supernatural constitutions as was the case with the creation of Lord Adam and the birth of Jesus Christ and revealed the consequences of making the wrong choice or undermining the rights and privileges of a real noble person.

A real noble person is a law lord from birth or creation, it should not be confused with political appointments associated with the political supernatural constitution, when it is said that someone will be a ruler rather than is a ruler. This is an important distinction because of the indirect regulatory functions or duties of a real noble person that start from birth or in the case of Lord Adam that started from creation.

In some cultures in Africa there is a distinction made between different rulers, the nobles are referred to as traditional rulers. The deception is that these traditional rulers are the real rulers; the word traditional is used to identify the civil noble constitution. It is an acknowledgment of the root of government, Lord Adam. This distinction has been reinforced by international and domestic legislations that define a legal person as the noble civil constitution without supernatural powers and senses. This definition has the effect of outlawing any type of political supernatural ruler.

Although these international and domestic legislations have got the wicked style or signature of supernatural beings with their misleading and confusing content, supernatural beings know that they dare not regulate real nobles because contrary to the delusion of some supernatural beings these legislations prohibit them from having direct or indirect contact or communication with real nobles.

I am of a civil noble constitution, a civil being, born in the United Kingdom of African origin, the Ibo tribe. I was taken back to Nigeria when I was about three or four years old, after a few years I was given a traditional title, Eze Okonko. No explanation was given regarding the significance of the title because at the time those around me supernatural beings were pretending to be of civil constitutions and were being misleading or confusing about the traditional title. It was when I returned to the United Kingdom and started becoming aware that those around me were different, with supernatural powers and senses, supernatural beings, that I figured out the meaning of the traditional title, translated to English it means king. Traditional ruler means lawful ruler. Traditional ruler or lawful ruler implies traditional or lawful reality linked to the traditional or lawful expressed civil rights of the civil noble lord. This differs from the false political supernatural reality responsible for organized crimes that caters to the natural sadistic nature of the supernatural constitution. This false reality is beyond the capabilities of the noble lord.

2. Witchcraft or Wizardry

The bible defines the lifespan of the noble constitution as immortality reinforced by international and domestic legislations that confirm that the noble civil constitution has the right to life. These international and domestic legislations also confirm that healthcare provisions must be made for the civil noble constitution implying that the civil noble constitution must not be harmed mentally or physically by supernatural beings.

Common law has gone further to make the determination that if there are any variations to the sacred healthcare provisions made for the civil noble constitution it is as a consequence of the unlawful misuse of supernatural powers and senses by supernatural beings and referred to as witchcraft and wizardry with severe consequences, punishment for the offenders.

When supernatural beings undermine any of the sacred civil rights of the noble constitution including the civil right to govern, any of the common law provisions made for the real nobles; their actions are regarded as unlawful and referred to as witchcraft and wizardry. This determination confirms that subjecting the civil noble constitution to the ageing process, old age, making the noble constitution ill mentally or physically, what they call diseases, it will be interpreted as unlawful supernatural attacks and referred to as witchcraft and wizardry.

The noble constitution has been constituted to rule to establish and maintain law and order; the needs of the noble constitution are sacred legal needs or legal rights for regulatory purposes. The rights and privileges of the noble constitution are sacred compensatory regulatory legal needs or legal rights. The undermining of these rights and privileges by supernatural beings is regarded by common law as witchcraft and wizardry.

Most of the command centres in science fiction movies or series are referred to as the bridge, this will suggest that law enforcement is about meeting the legal needs of the supreme commander the noble lord, law lord, without compromising the civil nature of the noble constitution. This involves meeting the compensatory regulatory legal needs of the civil noble lord who is sometimes referred to as a law lord which means legal civilized lord, the compensatory regulatory legal needs of the noble lord requires bridging the gap between the civil and supernatural constitutions in a civilized scientific manner so that the noble law should not be without and regulating the use of supernatural powers and senses because of the harmful effects of supernaturalism on the noble law and its disruptive effects in a civilized society. This has the sacred effect of creating and maintaining a real civilized society, paradise or heaven.

The indirect regulatory functions or duties of a real noble person start from birth or in the case of Lord Adam from creation and act as security sifting processes, supernatural beings are responsible for the production of food, they are required to produce food in a civilized legal manner and to make sure that it is safe and legal to eat. If it is not safe or legal it should not be produced. Why produce food that is not safe or legal to eat? Is it to test an already regulated noble constitution or an attack? Common law will interpret the production of unlawful or unsafe food by a supernatural being as witchcraft or wizardry an unlawful attack on the civil noble constitution. An example of unsafe production of food is the apple tree in the Garden of Eden. An example of an unlawful method and an unlawful food was when Jesus Christ supernaturally produced fish and bread. Fish is unlawful to eat.

Common law, international and domestic legislations, the bible have made predeterminations regarding the identity of the civil noble constitution based on the reality of the differences between the civil and supernatural constitutions. The civil noble constitution has been identified sacredly as ruler given the reality of what is possible. Supernatural beings have unlawfully undermined these sacred predeterminations in favour of delusional goals or projects that create hostile living conditions that are adversarial that are never ending that have the effect of making the lives of real nobles hell. This is regarded by common law as witchcraft and wizardry. This undermining of the law is linked to the desperation of supernatural beings, like heroin addicts, to cater to their wicked uncivilized constitutions. International and domestic legislations bar them, supernatural beings, from having contact directly or indirectly with real nobles not because they are above the law but because they are toxic, uncivilized.

Common law is very strict with its condemnation of witchcraft and wizardry, the misuse of supernatural powers and senses by supernatural beings to harm the noble constitution mentally or physically. It is impossible for the supernatural constitution to disassociate itself from its supernatural powers and senses during any contact or communication, the massive intimidating differences will most definitely create at least a mental effect on the noble constitution which will be categorized as a supernatural attack witchcraft or wizardry. The only solution provided by common law, are the rights and privileges of the noble constitution as king that counteracts the effects of the supernatural constitution, to provide the necessary sacred balance of power. This means that for the indirect regulatory authority of the noble constitution not to be undermined the direct regulatory authority of the noble constitution must be completely operational.

Common law, international and domestic legislations prohibit the use of the indirect regulatory authority of the noble constitution for any purpose other than for the establishment of a real civilized society which means to get the direct regulatory authority of the noble constitution operational immediately. The sacred motto in any real civilized society is that the supernatural constitution is not the solution but the problem.

Common law, international and domestic legislations refuse to accept supernatural beings in any relationship with the noble constitution outside the sacred determination that the civil noble constitution is king or ruler with the protocols, rights and privileges collectively providing a shield for the noble constitution from the uncivilized toxic nature of the supernatural constitution.

Regardless of the reasons presented by supernatural beings for undermining or compromising these provisions made for the civil noble constitution by common law and reinforced by international and domestic legislations, it will be interpreted as witchcraft or wizardry, the unlawful abominable misuse of supernatural powers and senses. Every conceivable situation has been taken into consideration before these provisions were made for the civil noble constitution by common law reinforced by international and domestic legislations, any deviation from these guidelines or instructions will be interpreted as deliberate unlawful attacks, witchcraft and wizardry. Common law, international and domestic legislations have a very simple method of identifying the noble constitution as ruler but supernatural beings want to undermine this for a more dramatic stressful method that suits the wicked nature of the supernatural constitution. Although the contents of domestic legislations are confusing and misleading the only relevant provision is the description of the noble constitution as a legal person protected by law.

These dramatic stressful unlawful supernatural methods always used or favoured by supernatural beings are why they are barred by international and domestic legislations from having contact or communicating with nobles. Common law offers the option of contact or communication with strict restrictions, these contacts or communications must be done always in the noble person's capacity as ruler with the sacred protocols. These sacred protocols offer the noble constitution the sacred protection from the uncivilized nature of the supernatural constitution. It is not the right of any supernatural being to undermine or take for granted this traditional or common law protection.

Common law has made the sacred determination that the violation or breach of these sacred protocols, sacred rights and privileges, to be witchcraft and wizardry the abominable misuse of supernatural powers and senses. This determination has been further reinforced by international and domestic legislations that only protect or identify the civil noble constitution and interpret violations of the sacred civil rights of the civil noble constitution as crimes against humanity. Common law provided the most horrific method of execution for the offenders as proportionate to their crimes against the civil noble constitution.

I am of a civil noble constitution, without supernatural powers and senses, a civil being; a spell was put on me collectively by supernatural beings that were hiding the differences between their supernatural constitutions and my civil constitution and torturing me mentally and physically at the same time for one unlawful political reason after another. Once I started becoming aware of the differences about fifteen years ago and the indirect spell they put on me started to wear off they put a more direct spell on me by supernaturally unlawfully altering my physical appearance including the shape of my teeth for unlawful political purposes that are beyond the civil noble constitution. This is regarded by common law as witchcraft and wizardry unlawful supernatural attacks on a noble lord.

3. A legal person protected by law

The bible made a distinction between the civil and supernatural constitutions in the Garden of Eden when Lord Adam was unlawfully compromised by supernatural beings and made to leave the comfort of the Garden of Eden. This same distinction and separation was made when Jesus Christ was born and distinguished from his biological parents Mary and Joseph. Jesus Christ was said to be the son of God a noble person although his biological father was a carpenter.
Common law also makes the distinction between the working class the supernatural constitution and the nobility the civil noble constitution.
The bible goes even further with its distinction by referring to the noble civil constitution as the righteous and the supernatural constitution as the unrighteous, wicked.
These distinctions by the bible and common law of the civil and supernatural constitutions indicate a refusal to tie the fates of both constitutions.
Alcoholic Anonymous is an organization that helps alcoholics recover from their addictions to alcohol. During their meetings the first thing an alcoholic does is to say his or her name and admit to the group that he or she is an alcoholic before speaking to the group. This applies to supernatural beings that must first admit to themselves that their supernatural constitution is hostile and antisocial. This will lead to the admission that they have the tendency to opt for antisocial uncivilized activities at the expense of law and order.
Supernatural beings believe that role play, pretending to be of noble constitutions is the solution, it is not. By their own actions they have confirmed that they are too wicked for that and will use role play as a weapon to harm the noble constitution mentally and physically.
Common law as a consequence has come up with what it means to be civilized for the supernatural being; it involves upholding the law by abiding by the sacred common law protocols when having contact or communicating with the civil noble constitution. Instituting the sacred rights and privileges of the civil noble constitution constitutes being civilized. There is a difference between a supernatural being

pretending to be civilized in order not to violate the sacred civil rights of the civil noble constitution and a supernatural being pretending to be civilized to abominably violate one or more of the sacred civil rights of the civil noble constitution.

International and domestic legislations do not take any chances with the security of the civil noble constitution, apart from barring supernatural beings from having contact or communicating with the civil noble constitution by not recognizing the supernatural constitution they have gone even further by barring supernatural methods of establishing relationships supernaturally with specific legislations. Examples of areas regulated by international and domestic legislations are the civil noble constitution's right to privacy, right to self-determination, right to freedom of expression, right to freedom of speech. International and domestic legislations that prohibit experimentation on the civil noble constitution, will interpret any deviation from common law protocols and the undermining of the common law rights and privileges of the civil noble constitution as violations of these international and domestic regulations.

To say that someone is born of God is another way of identifying the civil noble constitution, distinguishing civil beings from supernatural beings. This is because of the founding father Lord Adam whose original constitution was that of the civil noble constitution. It is not a claim to having any relationship with any supernatural being or supernatural beings but a distinction of the civil noble constitution from the family of gods as ruler, king. It is not a claim to having any special relationship with any supernatural being on the contrary, for supernatural beings to have any type of relationship with the civil noble constitution; it is dependent on the fulfilment of their sacred obligations to the state the civil noble constitution as ruler.

It is very important that the bible has gone as far as defining what recreation or playing is for the civil noble constitution, it is companionship with ladies and this must be formal which means that these companionships must be in the civil constitution's official capacity as ruler. This is as a consequence of supernatural beings that try to hide behind jokes and games to attack the civil noble constitution.

Parliamentary privilege (also absolute privilege) is a legal immunity enjoyed by members of certain legislatures, in which legislators are granted protection against civil or criminal liability for actions done or statements made in the course of their legislative duties. Diplomatic immunity is a form of legal immunity that ensures that diplomats are given safe passage and are considered not susceptible to lawsuits or prosecution under any country's laws. These are actually disability rights and privileges meant for the real ruling class the civil noble constitution. This is because the civil noble constitution is not criminally responsible, and has dominion over this planet whose movements should not be restricted by supernatural beings. These disability civil rights and privileges are extended to supernatural beings acting under the direct regulatory authority of the civil noble constitution.

According to the bible and common law, because of the way the real noble is constituted, a normal life is possible only under certain living conditions for the noble constitution which has never been accomplished. The tradition in the United Kingdom which might appear oppressive or domineering is actually disability rights for the vulnerable, which is a guide, the nobility always tend to live in luxury regardless of the state of a country and the working class in poverty. The civil noble constitution has been constituted in a delicate vulnerable way for sacred law and order purposes as ruler. Supernatural beings have sacred obligations to the noble constitution as ruler something similar to taxation but more advanced. The delicate nature of the noble constitution confirms that the civil constitution represents the immediate establishment of paradise or a real civilized society, here and now. No delay, delay is the style of supernatural beings that suit their wicked constitutions.

Supernatural beings have come up with different desperate methods to delay fulfilling their obligations to the state, the civil noble constitution, to the abominable extent of trying to refer to the civil

noble constitution as the devil. They collectively misuse their supernatural powers and senses to try to achieve this false abominable representation of the civil noble constitution.
Supernatural beings try to create false representations of themselves to the civilized, there are two problems with this delusion, the first is their sacred obligations to the state the civil noble constitution, the second is their supernatural powers and senses. This makes it difficult for them to claim ignorance to or not complicit in crimes against the civil constitution.
The supernatural constitution is uncivilized and has to behave appropriately to be law abiding including fulfilling their obligations to the state the civil noble constitution. The supernatural constitution is political, incomplete and needs approval to attain to any position. This makes the supernatural constitution susceptible to attacks on their credibility by their peers that want to undermine their chances of advancement in government positions and other situations. This becomes even more important than a peaceful society, making everybody's safety dependent on the personal ambitions of supernatural beings. This has become a way of life for supernatural beings which has created a mad world. This leads to attempts at the impossible, the abomination of discrediting the civil noble constitution for the personal political ambitions of supernatural beings.
The civil noble constitution as supreme commander represents a clear mandate, this makes policing efficiently straightforward which is boring for supernatural beings. They are not allowed to deviate from the mandate of the commissioner the civil noble constitution which is to protect the commissioner by regulating the activities of supernatural beings. The civil noble constitution has dominion over this planet and the mandate has the effect of providing protection for everyone including supernatural beings. The protection of the commissioner includes making sure that all the commissioner's compensatory regulatory legal needs or rights are satisfied.
For the protection of the legal consumer the civil noble constitution, international and domestic legislations have given legal boundaries to

products to protect the civil constitution the legal consumer from supernatural attacks or alterations. Examples of these legal boundaries are the images on television and the voices on radio, programming of computer games etcetera.

This is meant to protect the legal consumer the civil constitution from forced supernatural political exploitative relationships. This has been reinforced by international and domestic legislations with civil rights like the right to privacy, the right to self-determination, freedom of speech, freedom of expression, freedom from torture, freedom from experimentation etcetera.

The civil noble constitution has the right to life on the one hand a provision made by international and domestic legislations and on the other supernatural beings are barred from contact with the civil constitution suggesting that supernatural beings have failed in their obligations to the state with inadequate civilized healthcare provisions for unlawful sadistic purposes. A guide for supernatural beings is to be found in the science fiction drama series stargate sg1, the sarcophagus, not as a burial chamber but as a healing chamber that restores the body to good health regardless of the seriousness of the injuries or the state of the body.

Barroom brawls are conflicts with no rules with little or no provocation, this is the nature of supernatural beings, and this is why they like or favour hostile conditions. This is why they are barred by common law, international and legislations from direct or indirect contact with the civil noble constitution and direct or indirect communication with the civil noble constitution. They are too hostile.

4. Torture

When supernatural beings unlawfully undermine common law protocols concerning contact or communication with the civil noble constitution and the common law rights and privileges of the civil noble constitution, the effect on the noble constitution is torture in violation of an expressed civil right and recognized as a crime in the bible that triggers the civil noble constitution's sacred legal right of vengeance.

When a supernatural being has an unregulated unique interest in the civil noble constitution because the civil noble constitution is different from him or her it is torture because of what constitutes socializing for the supernatural constitution, which is fighting, whether the civil noble constitution is at a supermarket, in a taxi, accessing services or social security entitlements that the civil constitution has been unlawfully forced to get there are still problems because of supernatural beings unlawfully pretending to be legal persons. Their hostile constitutions betray them.

War is confusion; confusion is needed to feed their hostile constitutions. The comedy is that this is a sacred world and the clear mandate of the civil noble constitution given the nature of the civil constitution and the nature of the supernatural constitution, there are no opportunities for confusion.

Supernatural beings create confusion for the purpose of blinding the civil noble constitution to undermine the authority and mandate of the noble lord. They abominably make an objective or aspiration of a determination already made by common law, international and domestic legislations regarding the identification of the noble lord as ruler as if it had not been made to give supernatural beings something to fight about. This will require putting the noble lord in the middle of the insanity of supernatural beings exposing the noble lord to mental and physical abuse.

The bible, the Christian teachings, only recognizes torture as an acceptable type of punishment for the wicked, supernatural beings misusing supernatural powers and senses, because of the horrific effects of lawlessness on the civil noble constitution. The horrific effects on the civil noble constitution when supernatural beings undermine common law protocols when contacting the noble lord or communicating with the noble lord, the horrific effects on the noble lord when the noble lord's sacred civil rights are violated have been sacredly determined to be equivalent to the condemnation of the wicked, supernatural beings, to hell as described in the bible given the differences between the civil and supernatural constitutions including the psychological effects of their crimes against the noble lord.

Are supernatural beings sentient? I have to say no, they are not. They are too barbaric. It is not just that they are a threat to the existence of this planet and a threat to every living thing on this planet including real nobles, it is the method they use to inflict mental and physical harm, the level of sadism that is beyond torture. They must believe that they are overqualified for sentience.

As a consequence of the differences between the civil and supernatural constitutions every time supernatural beings undermine these sacred common law protocols and the sacred rights and privileges of a real noble person, whether they believe they are joking or not, playing games or not the resulting effect is serious mental harm and in some cases serious physical harm, which the Christian teachings interpret as unlawfully making the life of the noble person hell. These common law rights and privileges, common law protocols provide the necessary balance given the massive differences between the civil and supernatural constitutions.

Supernatural political role plays are only meant for supernatural beings. They are different ways supernatural beings harm each other, different types of self-inflicted punishments. The United Kingdom parliament consists of the nobility the House of Lords and the House of Commons the working class. It was a compromise reached for the working class to have more input in their affairs; traditionally they do not get involved in the affairs of the nobility. In reality these supernatural political role plays involve death, ageing, diseases poverty which the real ruling class, the nobility are in reality exempt. These role plays are beyond the capabilities of real nobles.

If you study the gang culture, gangsters will not want to show weakness to other gangsters even when faced with imminent destruction; it really is a political culture. The important educational information missed by supernatural beings is that gangsters really cannot defeat the state, the civil noble constitution. Hell as described in the bible as punishment for supernatural crimes against the state is undermined by the gangster mentality, as if they can handle it. It is effective and has all the necessary components which might not be noticeable initially because of the delusion that it is a gangster's paradise.

Supernatural beings might find it impossible to comprehend that the route to life and sentience is the noble constitution, the law. The state of the civil noble lord defines supernatural beings. The law is in living form as the civil noble constitution.

As a consequence of my experiences I can confirm that supernatural beings are naturally too hostile to make the needs of the civil noble constitution dependent on direct or indirect contact or communication with them. It makes no difference what type of relationship exists they derive pleasure from inflicting mental and physical harm. This is why international and domestic legislations refuse to accept supernatural beings in any relationship with the civil noble constitution. This is why common law has strict guidelines, the sacred protocols, for supernatural beings to contact or communicate with the civil noble constitution and the sacred rights and privileges of the civil noble constitution that create a protective shield for the civil noble constitution. Supernatural beings cannot and dare not undermine these sacred protocols, rights and privileges.

The sacred determination made regarding the condemnation to hell of the wicked for crimes against the noble lord is still in operation and cannot be changed by any supernatural being. This is as a consequence of the unlawful abominable undermining of the sacred common law protocols and the sacred rights and privileges of the noble lord and constitutes a deliberate unlawful compromise of the sacred protection of the noble civil constitution. The sacred legal right

Common Law

of vengeance of the noble civil constitution remains in operation.
A sacred determination has been made about the identification of the civil noble constitution as ruler, common law, international and domestic legislations have reinforced this identification by barring supernatural beings from contact or communication with the civil noble constitution outside this sacred predetermination. This sacred predetermination and the sacred constitution of the civil noble lord ensure that any contact or communication with the noble lord outside the sacred identification of the noble lord as king, king of kings, lord of lords, will generate allergic reactions from the noble lord that constitutes torture and every retaliatory punishment of the wicked in the bible constitutes torture culminating in the condemnation of the wicked to hell for crimes against the civil constitution. The reference to the civil noble constitution as lord of lords and king of kings is as a consequence of supernatural beings that are not real kings or lords because of their supernatural constitutions.

As somebody of a civil noble constitution I will exercise my sacred legal right of vengeance for supernatural crimes against me.

A vegan is someone who does not eat meat, fish, egg and dairy products or use products that were produced by abusing animals or the exploitation of animals. The current lawlessness in the world today suggests that all consumer products have been produced unlawfully as a consequence of the direct or indirect exploitation of the civil noble constitution by supernatural beings.

Every product or invention must be commissioned by the civil noble constitution as ruler; they must meet the sacredly recommended health and safety standards, usability, accessibility, durability etcetera. The civil noble constitution must be used as a measure to determine suitability and not the supernatural constitution. This sacred use of the civil noble constitution as the standard can be referred to as ruler.

The sacred purpose of the noble constitution must be sacredly compensated, not as a medical disability or as an inanimate object or as a ghost but as ruler, king.

The civil noble constitution is a law lord and a commissioner of the metropolitan police force; the salaries of both offices in the United Kingdom are about £600,000 a year. This in reality is very little compared to the private sector, but the state compensates for the shortfall by providing chauffeur driven government cars, government jets, government chefs etcetera.

Supernatural beings are a very hostile, aggressive species whether they are pretending to be civilized or not and as a consequence are forbidden from having direct or indirect contact with the civil noble constitution. The uncivilized wicked constitutions of supernatural beings was the reason common law developed strict protocols regarding contact with the noble constitution and established severe punishments for supernatural beings that fail to comply with these protocols. Common law confirms that unregulated contact with the civil noble constitution by a supernatural being is an unlawful attack on the noble constitution. Common law instructs that the differences between the civil and supernatural constitutions are not suitable for any type of interaction other than for the supernatural being to receive the instructions of the noble lord and to obey them.

My experience confirms that supernatural beings like to create hostile conditions, they like to establish awkward embarrassing moments to dominate meetings, they will go as far as putting a spell on you to compromise you by creating deliberately embarrassing situations in your life that they will make references to directly or indirectly. Fortunately the sacred protection of a real king shields the noble constitution from supernatural political emotions. The problem is that because of the natural retardation of the supernatural constitution they keep on trying to generate political emotions from a non-political noble constitution. The only effect is exhaustion rather than embarrassment because of their forbidden experimentations on the noble constitution.

Prostitution is the exploitation or the instigation of poverty, distorted physical appearance, protection, lack of credibility. In circumstances where credibility is in short supply or non-existent amongst a species, like supernatural beings, they rely on prostitution the use of force. Prostitution is the preferred culture amongst a species when credibility is non-existent.

It is more dignified for supernatural beings to associate a cause or an objective with the infliction and the receipt of pain rather than it being a natural craving like the fictional vampire's craving for blood. Living in denial limits the law's ability to domesticate supernatural beings. This deficiency in the supernatural constitution has led to the abomination of undermining the provisions made for the civil noble constitution by common law, international and domestic legislations, treating unambiguous legal entitlements as if they are ambiguous political ambitions or aspirations.

Try telling a species, supernatural beings, with this level of god complex and superiority complex that have interpreted the Christian teachings unlawfully implying that the reason for the separation is as a consequence of being superior and more civilized than the noble constitution, they represent an unacceptable threat to the noble constitution because they are too uncivilized. It will be like trying to reason with the Nazis diplomatically during the second world war to not only stop persecuting the Jews but that the Jews are their leaders or rulers.

Unfortunately these constant attempts to elicit political emotions have led to the disruption of my efforts to write, with the deliberate sabotage of the word processor tool, spell and grammar check, while at the same time putting a spell on me to make mistakes that the spell and grammar check tool in my computer should normally correct. The problem is that they overestimate their importance to a non-political real king.

Fortunately their supernatural attacks, attempts at sabotage, do not have any effect on the sacred judicial judgments of a law lord; it has the effect of activation of the official role of the noble lord as a law lord.

In a real civilized society the supernatural constitution is useless because of its disruptive nature and the civil constitution is useful. The challenge for supernatural beings to fulfil their obligations to the noble lord is to come up with scientific methods to detect, apprehend or arrest supernatural beings that misuse their supernatural powers and senses to harm mentally or physically the civilized or to breach the peace in a civilized society. Although it is not wrong to use supernatural powers and senses to detect, apprehend or arrest criminals until a more civilized method is developed scientifically. Supernatural beings do not have any civil rights. Some African cultures like the Ibo tribe use native doctors to detect supernatural attacks and to apprehend or arrest criminals. Criminals are supernatural beings that misuse supernatural powers and senses to harm the civilized mentally or physically or to breach the peace in a civilized society. The supernatural constitution is hostile uncivilized and is guided by its hostile or wicked counsel, as a consequence supernatural beings are barred from direct or indirect contact or communication with the civil noble constitution. Common law provides protocols that must be complied with for the protection of the civil noble constitution from physical or mental abuse. Common law rights and privileges of the noble lord operate as a shield and must not be taken for granted by supernatural beings. These guidelines have been reinforced by international and domestic legislations that do not acknowledge the supernatural constitution as a legal person for any purpose, or for any type of association or interaction with the civil constitution, whether as nurses, doctors, police etcetera. These professions could be used as weapons by supernatural beings following their own counsels deliberately to harm the civil constitution mentally or physically or as a consequence of retarded incompetence because of incompatible constitutions. International law defines a unique interest in an individual or a group of people that are different from the individual or group of people that have shown an interest that causes mental or physical harm to the recipients of the interest to be racist persecutory.

The deception about the hijacking of the attributes of the civil noble constitution by the conservative party as an ideology they commonly refer to as blue is a subtle type of sabotage. These attributes are self-reliance, individuality, traditionalism etcetera; they serve a sacred regulatory purpose when applied correctly to the right constitution, the civil noble constitution. When used by supernatural beings pretending to be civilized they serve a demonic lawless purpose. The common law protocols, the rights and privileges of the civil noble constitution when applied correctly to the real nobles they automatically create a sacred civilization police force under the leadership of the noble lord free from supernatural political manipulations or sabotage.

The blue ideology sabotaged by supernatural beings for their unlawful supernatural political role plays stolen by the conservative party, private enterprise or self-reliance or individualism is that supernatural beings cannot be monarchs, law lords, commissioners of police as alternatives to real nobles, these positions mean the same thing and are linked or connected to the civil powers and senses of real nobles the same way the supernatural powers and senses of supernatural beings are part of their supernatural constitutions. The salaries of these offices or positions have been assessed for the civil noble constitution.

The wicked unlawful interpretation of the Christian teachings by supernatural beings exposes the civil noble constitution to the unchecked unhealthy supernatural phenomenon and leaves the wellbeing of the noble constitution at the mercy of the wicked. This unlawful interpretation of the Christian teachings by the wicked involves the distortion of the interpretation of earth being part of the heavens and ensures that the fate of the noble constitution will be to end up in one type of hell or another including making the life of the noble constitution hell during the journey. The barring of supernatural beings from having direct or indirect contact or communication with the civil noble constitution is very serious, the bible and common law protocols forbid informal contact or communication with the civil noble constitution outside the civil constitution's official role as king. Undermining these guidelines constitutes torture with the retaliatory punishment described in the Christian teachings, the condemnation to hell of the wicked. This punishment is the retaliatory effect of the actions of the wicked on the civil noble constitution, given the massive differences between the civil and supernatural constitutions. Supernatural beings are not allowed to undermine the sacred selection of the civil noble constitution as king. Being a king has practical compensatory applications for the noble lord with the sacred result of establishing and maintaining a real civilization.

Supernatural beings are not sentient beings. Sentience is measured using the civil noble constitution. Supernatural beings have not got the ability to perceive hostile or dangerous situations or conditions and represent an unacceptable threat to the security of the civil noble constitution and the planet. This sensory failure of the supernatural constitution is the reason they are barred from direct or indirect contact and communication with the civil noble constitution by international and domestic legislations. Common law has made adequate provisions for the noble lord by establishing sacred protocols regarding the limited situations that contact or communication are permitted reinforced by the sacred rights and privileges of the noble lord. The undermining of these protocols, rights and privileges by supernatural beings constitutes experimentation and torture prohibited by international and domestic legislations. This will trigger the retaliatory punishment of the wicked as described in the bible. Supernatural beings are blind and can only see with the prescribed guidelines in common law, international and domestic legislations.

The legal principle that ignorance of the law is not a defence is based on the nature of the supernatural constitution and how the criminal law principle criminal responsibility applies to it. The supernatural constitution is naturally racist, the self-interest of the supernatural constitution does not have universal application but the self-interest of the civil noble constitution has universal application.

The United Kingdom legislation the Equality Act requires reasonable adjustments to be made to services, employment etcetera to accommodate the needs of the disabled, the common law protocols, rights and privileges of the noble lord are similar but in this case they serve regulatory purposes.

The sensibilities of the civil and supernatural constitutions are very different; the sensibility of the civil noble constitution has been sacredly determined to be sentient for regulatory governing purposes and the granting or the determinant of sentience in other life forms including supernatural beings.

When supernatural beings try to assume the sacred responsibility of the civil noble constitution it has the effect of torture for other life forms including the noble constitution.

5. Author's notes

The supernatural being is naturally very hostile like an undomesticated wild animal; imagine a wild animal with supernatural powers and senses that can stalk its prey supernaturally. The case of the supernatural being is worse than an undomesticated wild animal or the fictional vampire, in both cases they do it to survive but the supernatural being does it because of wickedness, they enjoy inflicting mental or physical harm. The undomesticated wild animal's need to eat other animals is as a consequence of the wicked sadism of the supernatural being, supernatural creation. The supernatural being will opt for a method that is hostile or try to hide behind help or concern to stalk their victims supernaturally. They will create situations that cater to their sadism even to behave like con artists fraudsters that try to gain the confidence of their victims. Lifestyles are established in what is claimed to be a civilization that in realty is a type of demonic organized crime that caters to the supernatural being. Living beings are created for the purpose of satisfying the wicked urges of supernatural beings. Never ending goals or objectives are established or created for the purpose of satisfying the wickedness of supernatural beings. As a consequence supernatural beings are not allowed to have direct or indirect contact or communication with the civil noble constitution regardless of the purpose by international and domestic legislations. Common law provides restricted circumstances when contact or communication can be allowed which require the expressed consent of the noble lord as king. The rights and privileges of a king are not for show they have sacred practical applications to protect the noble lord from the wicked nature of the supernatural being. An inventive way to cater to their sadistic urges is to make themselves appear to be victims of their victims.

The civil noble constitution has been sacredly restricted or regulated for a sacred regulatory purpose, no further regulations or restrictions of the civil noble constitution are permitted, and this sacred determination has a regulatory function. This determination implies that the noble lord cannot be restricted indirectly by being referred to as medically disabled because it defeats the regulatory function of the noble lord or financially by supernatural beings taking by force what is meant for the noble lord or by not fulfilling the sacred obligation to distinguish the civil constitution from the supernatural constitution officially as a law lord.

This book confirms that the law has made provisions legally for real nobles that are being undermined with the use of force by supernatural beings at the expense of making the lives of real nobles hell, this is a real unlawful supernatural political revolution.

This book also confirms that for lawless purposes rather than for regulatory purposes political parties in the United Kingdom have stolen the administrative tools of real nobles for supernatural political role plays. These administrative tools are part of the civil constitution in the same way supernatural powers and senses are integrated into the supernatural constitution. These supernatural unlawful role plays are beyond the capabilities of real noble, they do not have universal applications, they are discriminatory. These administrative tools have been divided by supernatural beings and used as ideologies for the different political parties in unlawful ways.

6. Author's biography

My name is Lord Loveday Ememe. I am a law lord of a civil noble constitution. I was born in the United Kingdom and of African origin. I am a graduate of an Anglican seminary school. I graduated from the University of East London with an honours degree in law.

Bibliography

The Bible

Wikipedia

Star trek drama series and films by Gene Roddenberry